You're never more than twenty feet from a Rat!
Encounters, Anecdotes & Tales
This edition published in 2004 by Advanced Marketing (UK) Ltd,
Bicester, Oxfordshire

Conception and compilation © Michelle Lovric 2004
Designed by Lisa Pentreath and Michelle Lovric
Editorial Assistant: Kristina Blagojevitch
Printed in China by Imago

ISBN 1903938635

10 9 8 7 6 5 4 3 2 1

Acknowledgements

With many thanks as ever to Iain Campbell and Judith Grant.
And a special thank-you to Fay Hogben for permission to use
so many items from her splendid archive.

The editor gratefully acknowledges permission to reprint extracts from the
following publications: *The Plague* by Albert Camus, translated by Stuart Gilbert
(Hamish Hamilton, 1948). Translation copyright © 1948 Stuart Gilbert; 'The Song
of the Pantegane in the Prisons of the Doge's Palace, Venice' from *Carnevale* by M.R.
Lovric, published by Virago Press. Copyright © 2001 M.R. Lovric; *1984* by George
Orwell, copyright © 1949 George Orwell. Reprinted by permission of Bill Hamilton
as the Literary Executor of the Estate of the Late Sonia Brownell Orwell and
Secker & Warburg Ltd.

AURA

You're never more than twenty feet from a Rat!

Pizon is good for rats,
what rats are good for I kan't tell.

Josh Billings (Henry Wheeler Shaw),
Josh Billings' Wit and Humour, 1874

There
they
go.
Patter,
patter,
scratch,
scratch.

Jim, the rat-catcher,
in W.A. Mackersy's play, *Rats*, 1898

You're never more
than twenty feet
from a

Rat!

Encounters,
Anecdotes
& Tales

compiled by
Michelle Lovric

Contents

Hark in the wall to the rat:
Since the world was,
    he has gnawed;
Of his wisdom, of his fraud
What dost thou know?

Ralph Waldo Emerson (1803–82),
American poet

More than any other
species of animal, the rat
and mouse have become
dependent on man,
and in so doing they have
developed characteristics
which are amazingly human.

Hans Zinsser,
Rats, Lice, and History, 1935

Introduction

For every human being alive in the world today, there is at least one rat. We have a humiliating amount in common. Both rats and humans are intelligent, resourceful and omnivorous. In both species, the males tend to be taller; the females rounder. Rats and humans make racial distinctions and war on their own kind, organizing armies when necessary. Both rats and humans mate all year round, but are thought to feel most amorous in the spring. We even share some of the same diseases.

If you look at things from a rat's point of view, we human beings are ideal companions. Our major investment, our pride and joy, our retreat — our home — comes to the rat unencumbered with housework or taxes, and our builders make sure they have plenty of places to hide. When it comes to eating, the rat likes what we like. So when we go shopping for food, we are also providing for rats. We dispense all the treats they desire, by our carelessness and our bad housekeeping. Our sewers are their temples. Our skirting boards are their pleasure domes. If they're in a nautical frame of mind, they can stow away on one of our boats.

We gourmandize our cats so they have no need to hunt rats. We've massacred their other natural predators to the point where rats rule the natural roost in many parts of the world. It could even be that by virtue of human-induced global warming we have made the world a better place for rats that used to perish in their millions in the cold winters.

Thanks to our *hyperactive imaginations, rats have become characters in important literary works and the stars of films. We have bred 'fancy' rats and pet rats. The Rat and Mouse Club of America alone has 100,000 members. There are even rats in space.*

And yet there is no animal that is more detested by humans. We are disgusted by the rat's pointed face, by its personal habits and its appetites. The rat is the incarnation of one of our deepest terrors: that of being eaten alive, or consumed in the grave. If we want to describe a human we despise, we go to the rat for our images and insults.

Where did we go wrong?

How did it come to this?

rats!

I don't give a rat's ass.

I
SMELL
A
RAT.

The Devil's Lapdog

Of all horrors in the world – a rat!
George Orwell (Eric Arthur Blair), *1984*, 1949

Rats evoke a universal shudder.
Cecily Barnes, American journalist

… for centuries a symbol of the Judas and the stool-pigeon, of soullessness in general.
Joseph Mitchell, 'The Rats on the Waterfront', 1945

Of all animals throughout the world none has made itself so universally detested.
Arthur R. Thompson, *Nature by Night*, 1932

In fact, the more we make ourselves acquainted with them, the more we seem to detest them.
The Piper of Hamelin, with other stories about rats, 1887

There's no denying it, all rats have an image problem.
www.RatRescue.org

… one of the most despised and tormented of created animals; he has many enemies and very few friends.
Francis T. Buckland,
Curiosities of Natural History, 1879

8

No One Loves a Rat

The mouth is situated a considerable distance
behind the snout, and the long, cleft upper lip
adds to its ugliness. The general effect of these
characteristics combines to make the brown rat a
most repulsive creature.

James Jenkins Simpson,
More Chats on British Mammals – Rodents and Bats, 1925

There is not even a fraction of utility or good to be
placed to its credit … it has no saving graces of
any kind.

James Jenkins Simpson

Its complete extermination
would be an unmitigated
blessing to mankind.

James Jenkins Simpson

Man and the rat will always be pitted against each other as implacable enemies.
Hans Zinsser

We are competing on this earth with rats.
Robert Corrigan, *Daily Ardmoreite*, August 2001

He is laughing at man's puny efforts to check his all-conquering progress.
Karl Gustav Anker-Petersen, *The Menace of the Death Rat*, 1933
The writer was the one-time manager of Rentokil

Everything is food to these filthy and audacious creatures.
Jean Henri Fabre, *Animal Life in Field and Garden*, 1926

They have no legitimate business.
Samuel J. Crumbine, *American Food Journal*, November 1914

Rats are bound by no other law than that of their own convenience.
Mark Hovell, *Rats and How to Destroy Them*, 1924

Its habitation is always associated with filth.
James Jenkins Simpson

The rat has gnawed its way into the very vitals of civilization.
Karl Gustav Anker-Petersen

… were he not a cannibal, he would long since have inherited the earth.
William Faulkner, *The Reivers*, 1962

You and I may be his next victim.
Karl Gustav Anker-Petersen

Rats in the Rafters

It is a curious, but nevertheless well-ascertained fact, that wherever there is a good habitat for a rat, it is quite certain that there a rat will be.

Francis T. Buckland

The house has far more inmates than the hosts
    Invited; cellar, pantry, kitchen, hall,
Are thronged with nibblers …

Elizabeth Akers Allen (1832–1911),
American poet

The Rat is the concisest tenant.
He pays no rent –
Repudiates the obligation,
On schemes intent

Balking our wit
To sound or circumvent,
Hate cannot harm
A foe so reticent.

Emily Dickinson, 'The Rat', 1875

The rats by night such mischief did,
Betty was ev'ry morning chid:
They undermin'd whole sides of bacon,
Her cheese was sapp'd, her tarts were taken,
Her pastys, fenc'd with thickest paste,
Were all demolish'd and laid waste.
She curst the cat for want of duty,
Who left her foes a constant booty.

John Gay (1658–1732), English poet

Neighbours from Hell

In the following extract, the author's father had unsuccessfully chased a rat around his library for hours and fallen asleep exhausted ...

In the morning, he was astonished to find something warm lying on his chest; carefully lifting up the bed-clothes he discovered his tormentor of the preceding night quietly and snugly ensconced in a fold in the blanket, and taking advantage of the bodily warmth of his two-legged adversary. These two lay looking daggers at each other for some minutes, the one unwilling to leave his warm berth, the other afraid to put his hand out from under the protection of the coverlid, particularly as the stranger's aspect was anything but friendly, his little sharp teeth and fierce little black eyes seeming to say, 'Paws off from me, if you please!'

Francis T. Buckland

All houses wherein rats and mice abide
Are haunted houses.
Elizabeth Akers Allen

Anything like the sound of a rat
Makes my heart go pit-a-pat!
Robert Browning, 'The Pied Piper of Hamelin', 1842

No one who has not been pestered with these
plagues can have any idea of the extraordinary
noise they will make. I have a most vivid
recollection of many sleepless hours during
my younger days, occasioned solely by the
gambols of the rats overhead.
John George Wood,
Sketches and Anecdotes of Animal Life, 1854

I 'ears them scamperin' round the walls
like newspaper boys with special editions.
Jim, the rat-catcher, in W.A. Mackersy's play, *Rats*, 1898

Rumble, tumble,

Flurry, scurry,
Now a rushing,
And a crushing;
Now a rattle,
And a battle;
Now a squeak
And a fall,
But the clatter,
For that matter,
And the rumble
And tumble
And scratching
And catching
Keep on
Through it all.

Rats in dozens,
With their cousins,
Or in droves,
With their loves;
Now it's raps,
Now it's taps,
Or it's crunching
Or munching;
Or a creak,
Or a shriek ...

Mary Mapes Dodge
(1830?–1905),
American poet

Rumble, tumble,

Everything You Didn't Want to Know about Rats

The word 'rat' has been in use in English for more than a thousand years. Some etymologists trace it back to the geographical origin of the species – Asia. Others refer to the latin verb rodere, to gnaw. The Romans themselves had no word for rat, although 'big mice' are mentioned in some texts.

Rats are now found throughout the globe, from the tropics to the Arctic and Antarctic. Buckingham Palace has a rat problem; in 1993 the White House acquired 165 unwanted rodent interns. After years of testing nuclear bombs on the Eniwetok Atoll, rats were still flourishing there. In 2003 the official National Rodent Survey found a population of 60 million Brown Rats in the United Kingdom, roughly equal to its human population. In America, latest estimates run to 1.25 billion rats.

The rats with whom we share our lives these days come in two varieties, Black and Brown. However, it is important to note that most 'Black Rats' are brown, and many 'Brown Rats' are black. Colour only becomes important after the species is identified.

BLACK RAT (*Rattus rattus*)

Other names and subspecies: Ship's Rat, Alexandrine Rat, Roof Rat, Old English Rat, French Rat, House Rat, Plague Rat, *Pantegana* (Venice).

...

Origins: southern or central Asia, India, Burma or Siberia. It is commonly supposed to have come to Europe in the eleventh or twelfth century in the holds of crusade ships but recent archaeological evidence shows the Black Rat was in Roman Britain. It proliferated alarmingly in Europe throughout the Middle Ages until the eighteenth century. Since then it has become rarer than its enemy the Brown Rat.

...

Description: up to 10 inches in body length; the tail even longer. Build: slender and elegant; sharp muzzle; large translucent ears (hairless). Soft fur intermixed with bristles.

...

Habitat: arboreal, or within the walls and roofs of houses. Dislikes water.

...

Famous for: transmitting the bubonic plague via a flea it shares with *Homo sapiens*.

The black rat is a more delicate and elegant animal and not nearly so repulsive in appearance.

James Jenkins Simpson

BROWN RAT
(*Rattus norvegicus decumanus*)

Other names and subspecies: Common Rat, Sewer Rat,
Water Rat. Wharf Rat, Norway Rat, Hanover Rat,
House Rat.

...

Origins: central Asia, possibly Chinese Mongolia.
During an earthquake on the Asiatic side of the River
Volga in 1727, swarms of Brown Rats swam over to
the eastern European side, reaching Paris by 1750,
and London even earlier, via trading ships from the
Baltic. Another story says that the Russian fleet brought
the species to Copenhagen in 1716. The name
'Hanover Rat' is a reference to the hated King George I.
His enemies said that he had brought the Brown Rat
with him when he arrived in England in 1714. It was
introduced into the United States in 1775.

...

Description: up to 12 inches in body length; same again
for the tail. Build: clumsy and heavy; blunt muzzle;
small furry ears. Being stronger, hardier, more fecund
and more ferocious than the Black Rat, it soon came to
dominate. A Brown Rat will generally kill a Black Rat.

...

Habitat: water – sewers, drains, docksides – and
earth, where it burrows.

...

Famous for: laboratory experiments (in its albino
form) and the infestation of most of Europe and
America. *Rattus norvegicus* is also the name of an
album by The Stranglers. It includes a track entitled
'Down in the Sewer'.

The brown rat is large and formidable …
disagreeable in its colour and appearance,
and vile in its habits.

Thomas Brown, *Anecdotes of the Animal Kingdom*, 1834

Oh, heavens! There runs a great big Norway rat,
Sleek as a banker, and almost as fat …

Will Carleton (1845–1912), American poet

Rats originally cum from Norway,
and i wish they had originally staid there.

Josh Billings

The rat is one of the most interesting animals on the
globe. In Europe he marks historical eras. Different
hordes of invaders brought their peculiar rat in their
train. Europe has seen the rat of the Goths, the
Vandals, and the Huns. Europe now has its Norman
rat and its Tartar rat; and the great rat of the Parisian
sewer is of recent date and Muscovite origin.

Alfred H. Miles, *One Thousand and One Animal Anecdotes*, 1903

Facts of Life

Rats are in heat approximately every 4 to 5 days
and can mate 20 times a day.
. . .
Gestation takes between 21 and 23 days.
. . .
Rats have between 4 and 7 litters a year, each of 8 to 14 young.
. . .
When the baby rats are 3 months old they can start mating.
. . .
Rats usually live 12 to 36 months.

Rats can:

Urinate up to 80 times and defecate up to 40 times a day.
. . .
Jump almost a metre (39 inches) upwards
and more than a metre horizontally.
. . .
Pass through any opening bigger than 1.3cm (1/2 inch) square.
. . .
Tread water for 3 days.
. . .
Fall 5 storeys without coming to harm.
. . .
There are more muscles in a rat's tail than there are in a human
hand. It can slip off the skin of its tail and escape if caught.
. . .
Rats do not vomit, and so they digest everything. Like all
rodents, they need to gnaw, in order to keep their ever-growing
incisors filed down. They can chew anything softer than their
teeth, and do damage to electrical wires, wood, lead and
aluminium sheeting, cinder block, brick, leather, cement, etc.
By gnawing through joists, foundations, telephone and
electricity cables and gas and water pipes they have caused
flood, fire and human death.
. . .
They can also eat the excrement of any other animal
as well as its rotting corpse.

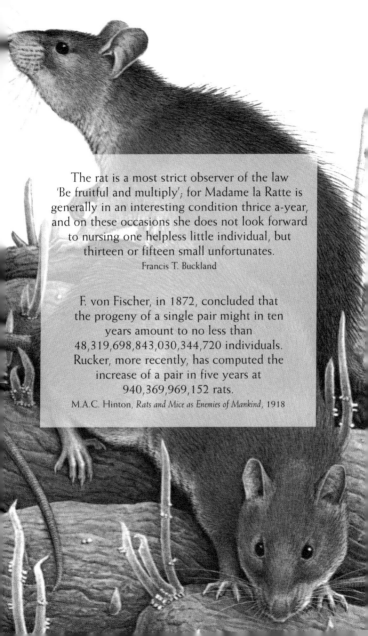

The rat is a most strict observer of the law
'Be fruitful and multiply'; for Madame la Ratte is
generally in an interesting condition thrice a-year,
and on these occasions she does not look forward
to nursing one helpless little individual, but
thirteen or fifteen small unfortunates.

Francis T. Buckland

F. von Fischer, in 1872, concluded that
the progeny of a single pair might in ten
years amount to no less than
48,319,698,843,030,344,720 individuals.
Rucker, more recently, has computed the
increase of a pair in five years at
940,369,969,152 rats.

M.A.C. Hinton, *Rats and Mice as Enemies of Mankind*, 1918

Years of the Rat: Find Your Inner Rat

The rat is one of the 12 emblems of the Chinese zodiac, even though the animal obtained his position by treachery. The rat and cat were supposed to go together to a grand banquet to decide which animals would be deified.

The cat took a nap in preparation, asking the rat to wake her. Thinking his own chances better without his friend, the rat left the cat sleeping and attended alone, to be selected for the great honour of a place in the zodiac. The cat and the rat have been enemies ever since.

Recent Years of the Rat:

1996
1984
1972
1960
1948

22

According to Chinese precepts, people born under the sign of the rat show a mixture of charm and aggression, outer calm and inner restlessness. They are level-headed in a crisis, alert to every detail, and great problem-solvers. They are hardworking and extremely adaptable, relying on their intuition to provide them with opportunities to better themselves. They don't like to be parted from their earnings. When the Chinese hear a rat scrabbling in the woodwork they say he is counting his money. Rats adore a bargain, and are sometimes tempted by unwise investments. They are hoarders. They are extremely sociable, and love large gatherings and small clubbish situations. In all things, rats are tribal and clannish, keen on secrets and conspiracies, and very inquisitive about the secrets of others. To their loved ones, they show a great deal of concern and involvement. Rats are avid readers — they love acquiring information — and make good writers.

Famous Rats: Plato, Tolstoy, Shakespeare, Mozart, Churchill, Washington, Truman Capote.

In 1984, the penultimate Year of the Rat, the Chinese government launched a massive rat cull in which an estimated 526 million rats were killed.

Archbishop Hatto of Mayence is the subject of a terrifying story that dates back to 970. In his second year as archbishop, there was drought and famine in Germany. Many families went begging at churches and at the gates of his palace. Not wishing to see his or the church's wealth frittered away on refugees, Archbishop Hatto rounded up 500 beggars in a barn, under the pretence of distributing food. But then he sealed the barn and set fire to it, killing everyone inside. He justified himself in a sermon claiming that beggars were vermin and should be exterminated like rats. Copies of the sermon were posted on the walls of all the churches.

Shortly afterwards, a great horde of rats swarmed into town. Archbishop Hatto fled to an island in the middle of the Rhine, and shut himself up in his so-called 'Mouse Tower'. But the rats swam out to the island, gnawed through the tower walls, and ate him. They then swarmed through the churches, devouring every copy of his sermon.

History and Legend

*Another traditional story, also recounted by the French poet
Jean de La Fontaine and much illustrated, is that of the battle
between the rats and weasels, here described in a poem by Anne
Finch, 1713.*

In dire contest the *Rats* and *Weazles* met,
And Foot to Foot, and Point to Point was set:
An ancient Quarrel had such Hatred wrought,
That for Revenge, as for Renown, they fought ...
Among the *Rats* some officers appear'd
With lofty Plumage on their Foreheads rear'd,
Unthinking they, and ruin'd by their Pride:
For when the *Weazels* prov'd the stronger side
A gen'ral Rout befell, and a Retreat,
Was by the Vanquish'd now implor'd of Fate;
To slender Crannies all repair'd in haste,
Where easily the undress'd Vulgar past:
But when the *Rats* of Figure wou'd have fled
So wide those branching Marks of Honour spread,
The Feather in the Cap was fatal to the Head.

The Pied Piper

The strange story of the Pied Piper, made famous by Robert Browning's poem of 1842, certainly has its basis in a real plague of rats in Hamelin in Germany. Browning's tale had a stranger arriving and offering to rid the town of all its rats for 1,000 pieces of gold. Promised this reward, he played his pipe and led an army of the rodents through the town and out to the river Wester where they were all drowned. When the townspeople failed to honour their promise of payment, the Pied Piper drew all the children out of the town, just as he had led the rats, and they were never seen again.

According to Browning, Hamelin (Hameln to the Germans) is in Brunswick but it is actually a town in Lower Saxony. Browning gives the date of the plague as 1376, but other sources claim that it happened much earlier – in 1284. Some interpretations have the rats symbolizing gypsies, others, the youngsters departing on one of the Children's Crusades.

Rats!
They fought the dogs and killed the cats,
   And bit the babies in their cradles,
And ate the cheeses out of the vats,
   And licked the soup from the cook's own ladles,
Split open the kegs of salted sprats,
Made nests inside men's Sunday hats,
And even spoiled the women's chats,
   By drowning their speaking
   With shrieking and squeaking
In fifty different sharps and flats.

Robert Browning

The story of the Pied Piper is still re-enacted every year in Hamelin and the town produces postcards to commemorate the event.

27

Rats in the Dock

A Lawyer's Head

In sixteenth-century France, rats were put on trial for their depredations …

This trial is famous in the annals of French law, for it was at it that Chassanée, the celebrated jurisconsult … won his first laurels. The rats not appearing on the first citation, Chassanée, their counsel, argued that the summons was of a too local and individual character; that, as all the rats in the diocese were interested, all the rats should be summoned, in all parts of the diocese. This plea being admitted, the curate of every parish in the diocese was instructed to summon every rat for a future date. The day arriving, but no rats, Chassanée said that, as all his clients were summoned, including young and old, sick and healthy, great preparations had to be made, and certain arrangements carried into effect, and therefore he begged for an extension of time. This also being granted, another day was appointed, and no rats appearing, Chassanée objected to the legality of the summons … A summons from that court, he argued, implied full protection to the parties summoned, both on their way to it and on their return home; but his clients, the rats, though most anxious to appear in obedience to the court, did not dare to stir out of their holes on account of the number of evil-disposed cats kept by the plaintiffs … The court acknowledged the validity of this plea … Chassanée gaining his cause, laid the foundation of his future fame.

Chambers' Book of Days, vol 1, 1863

There is one case on record, in Norway, of a colony of rats, while migrating in vast numbers from the high to the Low Countries, having been overtaken by a whirlwind; they were caught up, carried to a neighbouring valley, and there fell as a rat-shower.

Chambers' Book of Days, 1863

During the great flood of 4th September, 1829, when the river Tyne was at its height, a number of people were assembled on its margin. A swan at last appeared, having a black spot on its plumage, which the spectators were surprised to find, on a nearer approach, was a live rat. It is probable that it had been borne from its domicile on some hay rick and observing the swan, had made for it as an ark of safety.

Thomas Brown
This story has its parallel in La Fontaine's fable of the frog ferrying the rat across a river. A variant is illustrated here, interestingly, in a trade card for a corset.

Nineteenth-century Paris had a severe rat problem, too. However, Montmartre's famous Bohemian restaurant in the Place Pigalle, known as Le Rat Mort (The Dead Rat) was a gathering place for painters and poets, including Toulouse-Lautrec, Verlaine and Rimbaud. It was also famous for its gay clientele. Oscar Wilde once lunched there, 'extremely badly'.

In January 1993, the Nation *newspaper in Kenya reported the case of a Nairobi shopkeeper who walked into a police station clutching four large wriggling rats. He demanded that the police arrest the rats and charge them with ruining his bread supply.*

Rat Phobias

People fear being attacked by rats, as well they might. Women have a particularly fraught relationship with mice and rats.

'Great black fellows,' said one man, who managed a Bermondsey granary, 'as would frighten a lady into *asterisks* to see of a sudden.'

Francis T. Buckland

The psychological trauma inflicted by a wet rodent darting out of a toilet bowl … cannot be underestimated.

Brendan O'Malley, American writer

It utters a harsh metallic squeak when angry, striking terror into its assailant, while it produces a tremulous murmuring when amorous.

James Jenkins Simpson

Worst Fears

The biggest phobia about rats is that of being eaten alive, a theme taken up by many a B-grade movie. In Hollywood, it seems that a corpse is lonely without a rat. Vampire films always give rats at least a cameo role. Sometimes Hollywood rats grow to the size of dogs or cows on a diet of chemical effluent.

They have been known to … gnaw the toes off lepers too weak to resist, and to mutilate corpses in a mortuary; attacks upon … teats of live pigs are also recorded.

M.A.C. Hinton

The corpse of a man is not too dainty for this beast, and it always commences by eating out the eyes.

Alfred H. Miles

In 1556 the Italian poet Pietro Aretino succumbed to apoplexy after a fit of laughing. A priest dabbed holy oil on Aretino's forehead while performing the last rites. Breathing his last, Aretino turned to his friends and implored them, 'Keep the rats away, now that I'm good and greased up!'

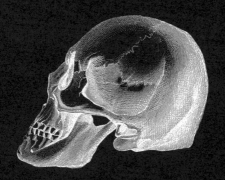

When impelled by hunger, rats migrate in large bodies in search of food, and then, with the additional courage which numbers give, they will not hesitate to attack human beings, as a Hertfordshire farmer received painful proof. One night, in crossing a common, he encountered a body of rats, a hundred strong. Though by throwing stones at them he endeavoured to prevent their purpose, they surrounded him, some of them running up his body as high as his shoulder, and inflicting severe bites, especially upon his hands … Rats are always found in coal-mines, securing the greater part of their living from the provender of the horses employed underground … Once … a pit was closed for a longer time than usual and the rats were reduced to starvation. The very first man who descended to resume work was attacked by the hungry horde, and killed and devoured before his friends could descend to his rescue.

Ernest Protheroe, *The Handy Natural History – Mammals*, 1909

In 1829, a rat bit three children, of a family in Exeter, two in the arms and legs, and the third in the throat. The rat was caught and killed, and its stomach being opened was found gorged with blood.

Thomas Brown

The refuse situation in New York grew to crisis proportions in the mid-nineteenth century. Rats moved in every night, devouring anything edible in the vicinity of the shanty towns, including cats and dogs. The New York Times of April 25th, 1860, reported a dreadful case of a woman found beside her newborn baby. The woman had given birth alone and had been too weak to drive away the rats that scampered all over her body. The baby was not only dead but had been mutilated by the rats.

The body of an unfortunate pauper, whose frame was emaciated to the last degree by famine and want, was brought to one of the theatres of anatomy in London for dissection. When the corpse was placed on the table, it was found that the whole of the lips and parts of the ears were wanting; in the place of the eyeballs were empty sockets; the parts also covering the palmar surface of the fingers were gone, only the bones and nails being left … in the space of one night live rats had committed all the havoc, devouring the most tender parts of the body; at least, I suppose they had found the parts that were missing were the most dainty morsels, for the marks of their sharp teeth showed that they had had a taste of nearly every other part of the body.

Francis T. Buckland

'Monsieur?'
'Hey?'
'Who was it that was eaten?'
'The cat.'
'And who ate the cat?'
'The rats.'
'The mice?'
'Yes, the rats.'
The child in consternation, dismayed at the thought of mice which ate cats, pursued:—
'Sir, would those mice eat us?'
'Wouldn't they just!'

Conversation between Gavroche and a young boy in Victor Hugo's *Les Misérables*, 1862

Pandering to this phobia is a 3D arcade game called Rat Attack, in which two evil mutant space rats return to Earth after 40 years in orbit. Death and destruction ensue as the rats of the world band together to establish themselves as the dominant species on the planet. To combat the rats there are the scratch cats, a crack squad of feline freedom fighters …

33

Everyone's worst nightmare is unveiled in this extract from 'A Legend of the Inquisition', a long poem by English writer Frederick William Orde Ward (1843–1922). The hero's beloved wife is devoured by rats, which then begin to eat him. His almost stripped corpse is able, however, to write the names of his murderers, which receive a just and dreadful revenge.

And he listened and listened, in breathless need;
But the feasting rats, they took no heed,
As they stript the frame in ravenous greed
Of the features that made it fair;
And when they were full, with emulous pace
Fresh troops poured in to take their place,
In the reeking fetid air.

And still they came in their hungry hosts,
They squeaked and moaned like gibbering ghosts,
And still drove in the outward posts
Of the army on the field;
They fought with frantic tooth and nail
For the dainty food, ere it should fail,
That none would lightly yield ...

In the blackness of that bloody strife,
On the shapeless thing that was his wife,
It seemed each rent was the butchers' knife,
And was driven into his frame;
It seemed as if for him they fought,
On him the devilry was wrought
That had no Christian name.

Each tap of the feet that darkness hid,
As a rat was gorged and downward slid,
Was the hammer's tap on the coffin lid,
From a hand that would not spare;
And the work went on, and the work went fast,
Till the awful meal was done at last,
And they picked the body bare.

And now was a pause in the dreadful deed,
While fresh rats gathered still to feed,
And still they came in their cursèd speed,
And they all had to be fed ...
But then they turned to the living man,
And on him once more fresh hosts began,
While they tore him shred by shred.

And the lean grew fat and the fat grew more,
As they revelled in human flesh and gore,
And they gnawed and nibbled, sucked and tore,
And ground as the millstones grind;
For they plucked the meat to the very bone,
As a dainty girl, though she has but one,
From the apple sheds its rind.

And they gouged his eyes and gauged his lips,
They clove to the cheeks with relentless grips,
And tasted his throat with greedy sips,
In their hunger great and grim;
And they rent him piecemeal, till the bands
They rattled upon his fleshless hands,
And they fastened on every limb ...

He felt no pain in the cutting pangs,
And there was no edge to the cruel fangs,
For his sense was dead as the life that hangs
Over the pit of death;
Though he knew the damnèd rats were there,
And rats and rats were everywhere,
And he drank their short sharp breath ...

And a fire within him seemed to burn,
As the embers in the funeral urn,
While fresh rats quarrelled for their turn,
For the flesh of man is sweet;
And they had starved and waited long,
They were mad for food and fresh and strong,
And the famine winged their feet.

In George Orwell's classic novel, 1984, the hero, Winston, has a phobia of rats. Confronted with them in Room 101, the place where all Big Brother's victims find their worst fears, he betrays his lover.

The door opened again. A guard came in, carrying something made of wire, a box or basket of some kind … It was an oblong wire cage with a handle on top for carrying it by. Fixed to the front of it was something that looked like a fencing mask, with the concave side outwards. Although it was three or four metres away from him, he could see that the cage was divided lengthways into two compartments, and that there was some kind of creature in each. They were rats.

O'Brien picked up the cage, and, as he did so, pressed something in it. There was a sharp click. Winston made a frantic effort to tear himself loose from the chair. It was hopeless; every part of him, even his head, was held immovably. O'Brien moved the cage nearer. It was less than a metre from Winston's face.

'I have pressed the first lever,' said O'Brien. 'You understand the construction of this cage. The mask will fit over your head, leaving no exit. When I press this other lever, the door of the cage will slide up. These starving brutes will shoot out of it like bullets. Have you ever seen a rat leap through the air? They will leap on to your face and bore straight into it. Sometimes they attack the eyes first. Sometimes they burrow through the cheeks and devour the tongue.'

The cage was nearer; it was closing in. Winston heard a succession of shrill cries which appeared to be occurring in the air above his head. But he fought furiously against his panic. To think, to think, even with a split second left – to think was the only hope. Suddenly the foul musty odour of the brutes struck his nostrils. There was a violent convulsion of nausea inside him, and he almost lost consciousness. Everything had gone black. For an instant he was insane, a screaming animal. Yet he came out of the blackness clutching an idea. There was one and only one way to save himself. He must interpose another human being, the *body* of another human being, between himself and the rats.

The circle of the mask was large enough now to shut out the vision of anything else. The wire door was a couple of hand-spans from his face. The rats knew what was coming now. One of them was leaping up and down, the other, an old scaly grandfather of the sewers, stood up, with his pink hands against the bars, and fiercely sniffed the air. Winston could see the whiskers and the yellow teeth. Again the black panic took hold of him. He was blind, helpless, mindless.

'It was a common punishment in Imperial China,' said O'Brien as didactically as ever.

The mask was closing on his face. The wire brushed his cheek. And then – no, it was not relief, only hope, a tiny fragment of hope. Too late, perhaps too late. But he had suddenly understood that in the whole world there was just *one* person to whom he could transfer his punishment – one *body* that he could thrust between himself and the rats. And he was shouting frantically, over and over.

'Do it to Julia ! Do it to Julia! Not me! Julia! I don't care what you do to her. Tear her face off, strip her to the bones. Not me! Julia! Not me!'

Rat Tastes:
Astonishing Voracity

As to its food, it were much easier to mention what it will not eat than what it does.

James Jenkins Simpson

The chief character of the Brown Rat is undoubtedly its astonishing voracity. There is no human food that it will not eat greedily. Provisions of all kinds are ruined, ricks and grain-stores are looted, hen-roosts are robbed of their eggs and young chicks, and rabbit warrens of their young. In the summer the pertinacious Rodent will betake itself to the fields, making its home in the hedge-banks, from which it issues to prey upon … almost anything that creeps or crawls that is smaller than itself. It frequently takes up its quarters in a river-bank, where it will contrive to catch fish.

Ernest Protheroe

Rats are not selfish animals: having found out where the feast is stored, they will kindly communicate the intelligence to their friends and neighbours.

Francis T. Buckland

Miss Henley told me a curious story about a barrel of treacle of her father's, which stood in an outhouse. To their great surprise, when they went to look for some treacle, they found the barrel empty. It appeared that some rats made a hole near the bottom, and inserting their tails, they then sucked them till all the treacle was demolished.

Lady Julia Lockwood, *Instinct, or Reason? Being Tales and Anecdotes of Animal Biography*, 1861

Some years ago the keepers at the London Zoo were puzzled by the restlessness of their elephants. The animals appeared very uneasy on their feet. A watch was kept and the cause was found to be rats, which came out at night and gnawed off the thick skin growing about the nails of the animals' feet.

Arthur R. Thompson

Many large animals are killed by rats. In the Zoological Gardens at Cologne two ostriches were killed by rats during the night. Once, too, fourteen rare Australian parrots belonging to my father were killed by rats at Spielbudenplatz in a single night.

Carl Hagenbeck, *Beasts and Men, Being Carl Hagenbeck's Experiences for Half a Century Among Wild Animals*, 1909

The vicinity of the slaughter-house of Montfaucon in Paris is so undermined with their innumerable burrows that the buildings there are in danger of collapsing ... They are attracted to these places by the abundance of food, the dead bodies of slaughtered horses. In one night, if left in the slaughter-house yards, dead horses are devoured to their skeleton. During severe frosts, if the skin is not removed in time, the Norway rats get inside the body, stay there and eat all the flesh, so that when a thaw comes and the workmen begin to skin the animal, they find inside the skin nothing but a host of rats swarming among the bare bones.

Jean Henri Fabre

Rats in New Delhi have been causing the police embarrassment by nibbling holes in plastic packets of moonshine liquor stored as evidence. When called on to produce the proof, the police have been unable to do so. Rats have also been eating vital police files on terrorism, murder and corruption, according to various newspaper reports in May 2003.

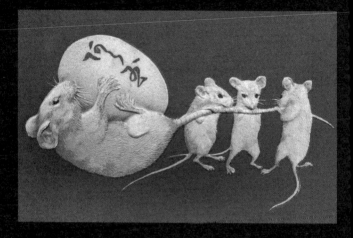

Do you know how rats steal eggs? ... two rats go together, one pulls out an egg from under the hen, and having done so, he lies down flat on his back holding the egg in his paws, and having thus transformed himself into a carriage, duly laden, the other rat pulls him along by the tail, and thus they carry off the egg, coaching away to their nest.

Lady Julia Lockwood

This behaviour is also described in one of La Fontaine's fables. However, modern science does not support this description.

The Rude Rat and the Unostentatious Oyster
(based on a poem by La Fontaine)

Upon the shore, a mile or more
    From traffic and confusion,
An oyster dwelt, because he felt
    A longing for seclusion;
Said he: 'I love the stillness of
    This spot. It's like a cloister.'
(These words I quote because, you note,
    They rhyme so well with oyster.)

A prying rat, believing that
    She needed change of diet
In search of such disturbed this much-
    -To-be-desired quiet.
To say the least, this tactless beast
    Was apt to rudely roister:
She tapped his shell, and called him – well,
    A name that hurt the oyster.

'I see,' she cried, 'you're open wide,
    And, searching for a reason,
September's here, and so it's clear
    That oysters are in season.'
She smiled a smile that showed this style
    Of badinage rejoiced her,
Advanced a pace with easy grace,
    And *sniffed* the silent oyster.

The latter's pride was sorely tried,
    He thought of what he *could* say,
Reflected what the common lot
    Of vulgar molluscs *would* say;
Then caught his breath, grew pale as death,
    And as his brow turned moister,
Began to close, and nipped her nose!
    Superb, dramatic oyster!

Guy Wetmore Carryl, *Fables for the Frivolous*
(With Apologies to La Fontaine), 1898

41

In this extract from 'The Three Tours of Doctor Syntax' written by William Combe in 1869, the eponymous hero wakes up in his room at an inn ...

He thought he saw a troop of cats,
But it appear'd that they were rats,
Who seem'd all frisking, quite at home,
In playing gambols round the room.
If they were fighting or were wooing,
He could not tell what they were doing,
But now it was his serious aim
To terminate this noisy game;
For to these rav'nous creatures, he
Had a deep-felt antipathy ...
He hiss'd and hooted, though in vain;
They fled, but soon return'd again.
To drive away this daring crew,
He with great force, his pillow threw;
But soon he saw them mock and scout it,
Running around and all about it.
The bolster follow'd, and a stool
Was sent their furious feats to cool,
And as a kinsman aids his brother,
The shoes, soon follow'd one another.
The night-cap too now left his head;
In vain the missile weapon fled;
In short the Muse's tongue is tied
To tell all that he threw beside ...

The ostler brings him two fierce cats to deal with the intruders, but the story is not finished ...

The morning came, th'unconscious sun,
Display'd what mischief had been done;

42

The rats it seems had play'd the rig
In tearing up the Doctor's wig.
All discompos'd awhile he strutted,
To see his peruke thus begutted …

The innkeeper swears he has never seen a
rat on the premises and Syntax replies:

'It is an animal I hate;
Its very sight I execrate:
A viper I would rather see,
Than one of this dire family.
That they suck eggs I may allow,
That they munch grain we all must know;
But I ne'er heard, I do declare
That these same vermin feed on hair.'

His servant Pat explains:

'No, no your Rev'rence,
Old Nick rate 'em,
They suck the oil and the pomatum;
And when in scrambling they grew louder,
O, they were fighting for the powder.
But still 'tis shocking, past enduring,
For the wigs maim'd beyond all curing.
– If they could have but eat the brains
Once cover'd by these sad remains,
And by a miracle been taught,
Just to employ them as they ought:
I know full well, Sir, what I mean,
Yes, yes, 'tis true, they would have been
The wisest rats, however droll,
That ever crept into a hole.'

Rat Eat Rat

Fortunately rats are ratophagous, eat one another, fight duels, indulge in broils and intestine feuds and grand destructive battles.

Alfred H. Miles

When other food fails, they kill one another, and it is a curious fact in the history of these animals, that the skins of such of them as have been devoured in their holes, are frequently found turned inside out; every part being completely inverted, even to the points of the toes. How this operation is performed, it would be difficult to ascertain; but it appears to be effected by some peculiar mode of eating out the contents.

Thomas Brown

Our bo'sun ... used to trap every six months or so, a dozen rats, kill the does and feed them to the bucks, after having first starved them for a while. He would probably repeat this until he had about six or seven strong bucks with a decided liking for rat-flesh. Then he would let them loose. I can tell you, mongeese weren't in it. They would begin with the nestlings and young rats and clear the ship in no time.

Tale of a sea-captain, quoted in A. Moore Hogarth,
The Menace of the Rat, 1929

Rats ... are very fond of fighting, and are addicted to cannibal habits. In the rat tribe, as well as among ourselves, the maxim that 'the weakest goes to the wall' holds good.

Francis T. Buckland

An animal so voracious is easily caught in a trap, especially when baited with roast beef, a food of which they are so fond, that they have been known to take out and devour the stomach of one of their own species, caught in a trap baited with this kind of flesh.

Thomas Brown

I once had three rats brought to me in a cage; in removing one it got hurt. I fed them, and put them into a stable. The next morning there were only two rats in the cage, the injured rat having been set upon and slain by his fellow-prisoners. They had not only slain him, but had actually begun to eat him, choosing the head to begin upon. Wishing to see the result, I left him, and in the course of the day, although well supplied with bread and milk, these cannibals had nearly devoured their friend.

Francis T. Buckland

You Dirty Rat:
Rat Poxes & Plagues

Dozens of diseases are carried by rats, or transmitted to humans by parasites we share with them. Consequently, it could perhaps be said that rats have killed more people in the past thousand years than all the wars and revolutions combined.

The present-day emblem of medicine, the snake-entwined staff of Aesculapius, refers to the use of the snake as a destroyer of rats.

The Black Death, or bubonic plague, has always been blamed on the Black Rat, but in fact the disease is spread by one of the many kinds of fleas that the rat hosts. Disastrous plague swept through the western world in the sixth century. A new plague arrived in Europe via the Crimea in the mid-fourteenth century. It spread in several waves, decimating the population. Nearly a third of all Londoners died in 1348. The plague subsided but did not depart, and came back with a renewed vengeance in 1665.

Domestic pets were suspected of being the cause and a great cull of cats and dogs took place. The plague spread even more rapidly without the natural predators of the rat to keep the rodent population down. The Black Death killed around 1.2 million people in Britain alone.

The Great Fire of London in 1666 purged the town of much of the crowded and unsanitary accommodation infested by Black Rats and their fleas. The old wooden buildings were replaced with stone and brick, presenting problems to the rats.

A bite from its filthy teeth
may occasion death in a few hours.

James Jenkins Simpson

Dysentery
TYPHOID
Salmonella
TRICHINOSIS
Rat-bite fever
Lassa fever
Rabies

Bubonic plague no longer devastates the world, but rats still stand accused of spreading many other diseases: Typhoid, Rat-bite fever, also known as Sodoku, Leptospirosis/Spirochaetal jaundice, also known as Weil's disease, Salmonella, Dysentery, Hanta virus, Rabies, Russian spring-summer encephalitis, Lassa fever, Trichinosis.

Whether both the Brown Rat and the Black Rat carry the bubonic plague fleas is a source of discussion amongst scientists. Traditionally only the Black Rat is blamed.

Our dread of the rat as a mere animal is inexplicable, but in the light of a transmitter of diseases the hatred of this rodent is more readily understood.

Sir James Cantlie, 'The Part Played by Vermin in the Spread of Disease', 1909

A rat flea feeds on the blood of a rat infected with the plague germ Bacillus pestis, ingesting up to 5,000 germs in one meal. The germs multiply so rapidly in the flea's stomach that a cluster obstructs the entrance to its gullet. The flea continues to feed, sucking blood from its host, but the obstruction in its alimentary canal prevents it from swallowing, and so the blood is forced back into the wound. Eventually the sick rat dies, and the flea has to find another host — a rat or a man — to feed on. The flea then bites and pumps blood repeatedly, pushing infected blood back into the body of the new host and thereby contaminating it with plague germs. A single germ is enough to kill a man.

Recently the Health Department of the city of Providence, Rhode Island, examined 341 rats for the numbers of fleas upon them ... the average number of fleas per rat being 11, and the largest number of fleas on any single rat being 300.

Samuel J. Crumbine, *American Food Journal*, November 1914

Plague and rat necessarily are inseparable.

Dr Louis Sambon, *Journal of Tropical Medicine and Hygiene*, June 1924

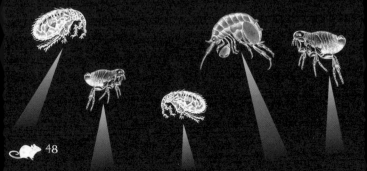

A Modern Plague

On the fourth day the rats began to come out and die in batches. From basements, cellars and sewers they emerged in long wavering files into the light of day, swayed helplessly, then did a sort of pirouette and fell dead at the feet of the horrified onlookers. At night, in passages and alleys, their shrill little death-cries could be clearly heard. In the mornings the bodies were found lining the gutters, each with a gout of blood, like a red flower, on its tapering muzzle; some were bloated and already beginning to rot, others rigid, with their whiskers still erect … People out at night would often feel underfoot the squelchy roundness of a still warm body. It was as if the earth on which our houses stood were being purged of its secreted humours — thrusting up to the surface the abscesses and pus-clots that had been forming in its entrails.

Albert Camus, *The Plague*, 1947

I Smell a Rat: Rat Expressions

I smell a rat.
There is something suspicious going on.

I don't give a rat's ass.
I don't care at all.

To rat on someone.
To betray them.

Rat hole
A horrible, dirty, dark dwelling.

Like two rats in a rat trap.
A couple that doesn't get on.
Noël Coward, *The Rat Trap*, 1918

The Rat Race
The world of human struggle and competition.

Ratfink!
Evil-doer

Rats!
Oh no!

You dirty rat!
You criminal betrayer!
(apocryphally attributed to the actor James Cagney)

There's a rat in your fore-chains.

The ultimate insult for a dirty ship, in old naval parlance.

Frank C. Bowen, *Sea Slang*, 1929

Rat Pack

A group up to no good, usually applied to Dean Martin, Sammy Davis Junior and Frank Sinatra.

King of the Rats

A leader who uses his wits to survive on the labour of less clever slaves, as in James Clavell's 1962 novel, *King Rat*, about a prisoner-of-war camp in Japanese-occupied Singapore during the Second World War.

Avoir les rats morts.

Literally, to have a case of the dead rats: to be depressed.

A favourite expression of the Duke of Wellington, when people tried to coax him to do what he had resolved not to do, was 'The rat has got into the bottle'. This not very intelligible expression may refer to an anecdote I have heard of the Duke's once telling, in his later days, how the musk-rats in India got into bottles, which ever after retained the odour of musk.

Adam White, *Heads and Tales*, 1870

On January 25th, 2002 a Brown Rat crossed the floor of the House of Commons in the middle of a debate. One MP quipped, 'I smell a rat in this legislation.' The Daily Telegraph's political correspondent, Jon Hibbs, remarked, 'MPs could not tell which sinking ship it was leaving.'

The trouble with the rat race is that if you win you're still a rat.

Lily Tomlin (b. 1939), American actress

Rat Proverbs
and Superstitions

A sudden increase in the number of rats presages war.

. . .

If you see rats leaving a building, it will soon burn or collapse.

. . .

Rats chewing furniture is an omen of death.

. . .

*It is a sign of good luck to have a rat
jump out of a drawer that you have opened.*

. . .

Rats will desert a doomed ship.

. . .

*You should never mend any clothes that a rat has gnawed,
for it will bring you bad luck.*

. . .

Anyone who eats rat-gnawed food will
be falsely accused of wrongdoing.

Mexican superstition

. . .

*In the Pacific island of Raratonga, when a child lost
a milk tooth, this prayer would be recited:*

Big rat! Little rat!
Here is my old tooth.
Pray give me a new one.

*The tooth would then be thrown on the thatch roof of the house,
as that was where the rats would nest. The Raratongans
prayed to the rat as they believed that rats' teeth
were the strongest.*

. . .

*In Germany, people put children's milk teeth in mouse holes to
prevent their children from getting toothache.*

'Speaking of rats, once in Honolulu me and old Josephus … were going home as passengers from the S.I. in a brand-new brig on her third voyage – and our trunks were down below … There was a wood-pile right where the line was made fast to the pier, and up come the damndest biggest rat – as big as an ordinary cat he was – and darted out on that line and cantered for the shore – and up came another – and another – and another – and away they galloped over that hawser … they never let up till the last rat was ashore out of that brand-new beautiful brig. I called a Kanaka with his boat, and he hove alongside and shinned up a rope and says I: "Do you see that trunk down there?" "Ai." "Clatter it ashore as quick as God'll let you."

'Josephus, the Jew, says: "What are you doing, Captain?" and I says: "Doing? Why I'm a-taking my trunk ashore, that's what I'm-a-doing!"

'"Taking your trunk ashore? Why bless us what is that for?"

'"What is it for?" says I – "Do you see them rats? Do you notice them rats a-leaving this ship? She's doomed, Sir – she's doomed! Burnt brandy wouldn't save her, Sir! She'll never finish this voyage. She'll never be heard of again, Sir."

'Josephus says: "Boy, take that other trunk ashore too."

'And don't you know, Sir, that brig sailed out of Honolulu without a rat aboard and was never seen again by mortal man, Sir. We went in an old tub, so rotten that you had to walk easy on the main deck to keep from going through … and the rats were as big as greyhounds and as lean, Sir, and they bit the buttons off of our overcoats and there were so many of them that in a gale once they all scampered to the starboard side when we were going about and put her down the wrong way, so that she'd come monstrous near foundering! But she went through safe, I tell you, because she had rats aboard.'

Captain Ned Wakeman in Mark Twain (Samuel Langhorne Clemens), *Notebook*, 1935

53

Man Eats Rat

The rat is the only animal that SAS officers on field training are forbidden to eat: it is too unhealthy. In the Bible both *Leviticus* and *Isaiah* define the mouse or rat as an unclean 'creeping' animal and not fit for consumption. However, Pliny suggests in his Natural History that a woman who wants a dark-eyed baby should eat a rat while she is pregnant. Upton Sinclair's 1906 novel, The Jungle, warned that people who ate sausages were liable to consume dead rats that were among the factory sweepings fed into the conveyor belt in meat-packing factories. People have hunted rats for food in times of scarcity, a good way of keeping down the population. In China, the homeland of the rat, a soup has traditionally been made from the rodent. When Paris was under the Prussian siege in the 1870s, rats even appeared on the menus of fashionable restaurants. A book called Wild Food of Britain, still being sold in the 1920s, included a rat recipe.

Traps were set for rats, which were consumed in such numbers that ere the termination of the siege, they actually became a scarcity.
Hunger will demoralize the most fastidious tastes … The author made a hearty breakfast on fried rats, whose flesh he found very good.

W.H. Tunnard, American Civil War soldier

… Rats become dainties where God sends a famine.

John Williams (1761–1818), English poet

Of course, rats might form a cheap source of food. They have been eaten without harm under stress – at the siege of Paris in 1871, and before that by the French garrison at Malta in 1798, where, according to Lantz, food was so scarce that a rat carcass brought a high price.

Hans Zinsser

Right now as I am writing these words there is a rat vendor going along the street carrying three large rats by the tail, and every few steps I hear him cry: 'Here are your rats, fresh and fat! I just now caught them at the commissary department, and I warrant them to be in fine order. Three for five cents, cheap! Here are your rats!' … I have been hungry for six months now, and I could and would eat a rat or snake on toast if I just had it.

George Michael Neese, American Civil War soldier

When that gallant sailor Rear-Admiral Beaufort was making a cruise in H.M.S. *Woolwich*, his ship was swarmed with rats … Determined to get over the silly prejudice against such animals, as they fed on his peas and flour, he ordered those that were killed to be brought to his steward for selection, and he reports that the old grizly ones were very strong, but that spatchcocked and broiled, with plenty of salt and pepper, the head quarters were really not bad; but prejudice was stronger even than rats, and no one, either young or old, could get down a mouthful without a long face.

Francis T. Buckland

In western society the idea of eating a rat conjures only horror, as when Bette Davis tortures Joan Crawford by serving her a rat for lunch in an unforgettable scene in the film Whatever Happened to Baby Jane?

In Asia it is different. On May 31st, 1991 the Wall Street Journal reported on a restaurant in Guangzhou, China, that specializes in rat dishes, with more than thirty on the menu, including Black Bean Rat, Rat with Chestnut and Duck, Lemon Deep Fried Rat, Satayed Rat Slices with Vermicelli, Liquored Rat Flambé, German Black Pepper Rat Knuckle, a Nest of Snake and Rat, Vietnamese Style Rat Hot Pot, a Pair of Rats Wrapped in Lotus Leaves, Salted Rat with Southern Baby Peppers, Salted Cunning Rats, Fresh Lotus Seed Rat Stew, Seven-Colour Rat Threads, Dark Green Unicorn Rat – and, of course, Classic Steamed Rat, and Rat Kabob.

The restaurant is named Jialu, which translates as 'Better than Deer'. All the rats are free range. Customers are not lacking, though some warn that the meat is very rich, raises the body temperature, and can even cause nose-bleeds. On the plus side, eating rats, the owner claims, helps to prevent hair loss, raise libido, arrest senility and alleviate stress. Even the Chinese government promotes rat meat as good eating. The official line is that 'rats are better looking than sea 'slugs and cleaner than chickens and pigs'.

The body was impaled on a long wooden skewer, and turned briskly round over a fierce fire, until the hair was completely burnt; it was then scraped with a sharp piece of wood, until free from fur, and of a rich, toasty, brown colour … When I expressed surprise that he could eat such food, Inkle would reply with a merry grin, 'Ki? nyoung massa, ratta sweet, hearee?'

The Reverend Bowater Vernon describes how a slave prepared his evening meal in *Early Recollections of Jamaica*, 1848

Other Uses of a Dead Rat

An ingenious individual of Liskeard, Cornwall, has for some time past been exhibiting himself in a dress composed from top to toe of rat-skins, which he has been collecting for three years and a half … It consists of hat, neckerchief, coat, waistcoat, trousers, tippet, gaiters, and shoes. The number of rats required to complete the suit was 670 …

Francis T. Buckland

It has, indeed, been asserted that large numbers of 'kid' gloves were made from the skins of rats caught in the catacombs and sewers of Paris.

The Piper of Hamelin, with other stories about rats, 1887

Even the fur of the Brown Rat has its uses. During the Russo-Japanese war of 1905, the Japanese warded off frostbite by using rat-skins as ear-caps.

The Scottish engineer and inventor James Watt gave advice on minor engineering matters, too: he advised a celebrated Swedish artist to use rats' whiskers for paintbrushes, as they were the most pliant and elastic materials possible.

The Rats of War

The carnage of the First World War was just fresh food for the rat population of the trenches. Rats fattened on the corpses of fallen soldiers grew so big and bold that they would attack a wounded man, or rifle the pockets of sleeping ones.

There were rats, rats, big as bloody cats
In the store, in the store.
There were rats, rats, big as bloody cats
In the Quartermaster's store.

Traditional soldiers' song

The rats here are particularly repulsive, they are so fat – the kind we call corpse-rats. They have shocking, evil, naked faces, and it is nauseating to see their long, nude tails.

Erich Maria Remarque, *All Quiet on the Western Front*, 1929 .

The darkness crumbles away
It is the same old druid Time as ever,
Only a live thing leaps my hand,
A queer sardonic rat,
As I pull the parapet's poppy
To stick behind my ear.
Droll rat, they would shoot you if they knew
Your cosmopolitan sympathies,
Now you have touched this English hand
You will do the same to a German
Soon, no doubt, if it be your pleasure
To cross the sleeping green between.
It seems you inwardly grin as you pass
Strong eyes, fine limbs, haughty athletes,
Less chanced than you for life,
Bonds to the whims of murder,
Sprawled in the bowels of the earth,
The torn fields of France.

Isaac Rosenberg, 'Break of Day in the Trenches', 1916

Am I myself a rat? I gnaw my slice
Of bread with a rat's teeth. There are no things
Beyond this cell. Naught is, save rats and mice.

Eugene Jacob Lee-Hamilton, 'Latude to his Rats', 1750

The Walls embelisht with the Slime
Of Snails, which winding upward climb:
In ev'ry Corner of the Room
A Spider working at her Loom:
Visits from Courteous Rats and Mice,
Millions of Philanthropick Lice,
Unwillingly will meet abstersion
From close adherence to your Person:
With great variety of swarming
Insects, and pretty sort of Vermin.

Anonymous description of a vermin-ridden prison cell,
Minor Burlesques and Travesties, 1698

Ships' Rats

For centuries the most troublesome of
stowaways on a ship have been rats ... In
addition to destroying cargo, they often, when
in harbour, escape into the warehouses and
dwellings in or near the docks, and if infected
may easily cause an outbreak of plague. Rats
gain access to the shore by means of gangways,
ropes and hawsers. Gangways should be watched and
only one gangway should be down at a time when not
in actual use.

A. Moore Hogarth

On board a man-of-war they have been known to
consume a hundredweight of biscuits daily, and when,
to destroy them, the ship has been smoked between
decks, six hampers a-day have for some time been
filled with their carcasses.

George-Louis Leclerc, Comte de Buffon, *Natural History of Beasts, Birds,
Fishes and Insects*, 1864

There was an army of rats travelling with us, and the
very first morning I awoke to find that a hole had been
gnawed by them in my friend Mlle Guillou's skirt,
which had been hung on a peg ... during the whole
voyage they kept us company, subsequently, however,
confining their attention to the peaches I purposely
placed within their reach.

Lillie Langtry, *The Days I Knew*, 1925

When the ship Pamir *was disinfested in 1949, from that single
vessel were brought forth the corpses of nearly 8,000 rats. The
boat had served as a floating grain store at Penarth in Wales.*

During the war … [the Black Rat] was common in certain parts of H.M.S. *Dreadnought* … With a ship's company of nearly a thousand, these rats learned to  live very secretive lives. Gnawing a steel battleship was out of the question, but the rats were exceedingly clever in utilizing any place affording safety and food. Most of them lived 'mid-ships in the hydraulic pump room containing the immense drums around which were coiled the main purchase and topping lift hawsers of the main derrick. Their home was actually amid machinery which, when it was in motion, created a tremendous uproar. The bulk of food must have been greases, with variations provided by occasional very risky nocturnal excursions to other parts of the ship.

Arthur R. Thompson

Another article of diet less inviting at first, but which I found more innocuous [than bears' liver], was the rat … Their impudence and address increased with their numbers; it became impossible to stow anything below decks … Before the winter ended I avenged our griefs, by decimating them for my private table. If I was asked what, after darkness, and cold, and scurvy, are the three besetting curses of our Arctic sojourn, I should say rats, rats, rats.

Elisha Kent Kane (1820–57), American physician and explorer

Venetian Rats

The rats of Venice are famous in literature and film, notably Indiana Jones and the Last Crusade. The Venetians have their own name for the animal: pantegana.

The pantegane of Venice are celebrated by fashion designer Fiorella Mancini, at her eye-catching shop in Campo Santo Stefano. The designer paints luminous green rats on her sumptuous velvet clothes. One Carnevale a few years ago, Fiorella (a household name in Venice) went down the Grand Canal in a boat refashioned as a giant water rat.

The Sea Rat in Kenneth Grahame's The Wind in the Willows, 1908, is overcome with dreamy nostalgia when he recalls his visit there: 'O, Venice is a fine city, wherein a rat can wander at his ease and take his pleasure!' He goes on to describe the pleasures of feasting with friends on the edge of the Grand Canal on starry nights. Indeed, they may still be seen there, doing just that.

Venice does not return the Sea Rat's affection. There is a legend that the famous cats of Venice were imported from Syria to cull the rat population. Cats are fewer nowadays, and the town's current derattizatore performs derattizazione with poison every day.

One famous rat-hater was Venice's native son, Casanova, who, imprisoned in the Doge's Palace in 1755/6, recalled rats as big as rabbits running over his head at night. This poem about the rats in the Doge's Palace, written in their own supposed dialect, comes from the editor's novel about Casanova, Carnevale, published in 2001:

The Song of the Pantegane

The culls come in all aflourish in their lace
They're bacon-fed and pasta-gutted
Silk waistcoats stretched over tripes and trullibubs
Stale drunk, tears of the bottle on their frock-coats
Pink and breathless from the pushing shop or
Trowser-ripe from lying in state with their regular harlots.
They think they'll soon be out. Ha!

It's not long before they're
Dancing like death's head on a mopstick
Herring-gutted, weasel-faced,
Scratching at their scrubbados
And clutching at their eelish paunches,
Screaming that their great guts are ready to eat their little ones.

Some girls plead their bellies
But all the morts stop bleeding here.
Their fur drops off: they rub their nude pimply pelts.
Soon they stop talking, or mumble like a mouse in a cheese.
By then they all whiff the same, or more so.
So in the end we only know the fresh ones from the stale ones
And the dead ones from the dying.

You think we'd woffle 'em? Sniv that!
A wolf in the stomach would not persuade us!
We'd rather sail to the spice-islands in a privy-pot!…

We draw the line in Rat-land
Nothing rotten, kickerpoo or still crawling or
Too damned sad on our red rags, our tongues.
Misery stinks most confoundedly.
Anyway there's too much competition
From the active citizens, by which I mean
the lice, the fleas, the flies and the mosquitoes.
They're sharp, the jointed beasts.
They know their trade.
They start eating
Before the jailbirds are even dead.

Library Rats: Rats in Books

Rats are great consumers of literature, unfortunately in a literal sense. There are many poems and anecdotes about rats eating precious books and manuscripts and even art.

In Juvenal's Third Satire, here translated by John Dryden, Codrus, a poor but learned man has his collection of Homer eaten by rats:

> His few Greek books a rotten chest contained,
> Whose covers much of mouldiness complained;
> Where mice and rats devoured poetic bread,
> And with heroic verse luxuriously were fed.

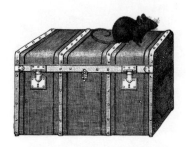

The incomparable ornithologist and artist Audubon went on a journey from Kentucky to Philadelphia. In the meantime, he had all his bird drawings sealed up carefully in a wooden box. On his return he opened the box to find that a pair of Norway rats had moved in and had brought up a young family amongst the gnawed bits of paper – those same pieces of paper that had once been his exquisite paintings of birds. It is reported that Audubon literally swooned with horror at the devastation of his work, but set to recreating it immediately.

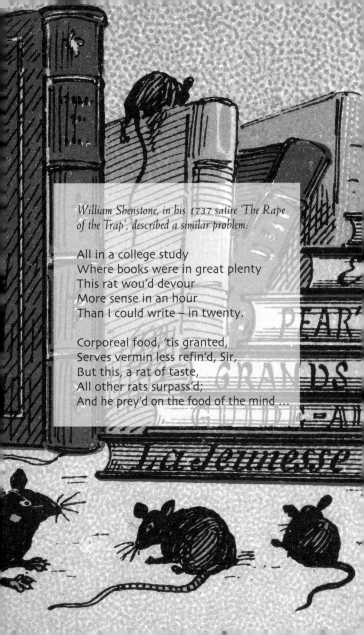

William Shenstone, in his 1737 satire 'The Rape of the Trap', described a similar problem:

All in a college study
Where books were in great plenty
This rat wou'd devour
More sense in an hour
Than I could write – in twenty.

Corporeal food, 'tis granted,
Serves vermin less refin'd, Sir,
But this, a rat of taste,
All other rats surpass'd;
And he prey'd on the food of the mind ...

Jean de La Fontaine (1621–95) wrote several fables about rats – some based on Aesop's – establishing the creature as cunning, ruthless and at times, over-ambitious. The stories include:

'The City Rat and the Country Rat' (the boastful city rat is trounced by his humble country cousin)

'The Council Held by Rats' (in which the rats decide to hang a bell around the neck of a troublesome cat. It's a great idea, but who will do it?)

'The Lion and the Rat' (the lion spares the rat; the rat later saves the lion from captivity by gnawing his ropes)

'The Cat and the Old Rat' (a cat pretends to be dead, to lure young rats to their death)

'The Battle of the Rats and the Weasels' (see page 25)

'The Frog and the Rat'
(a perfidious rat attempts to play a foul trick on a kind frog, but fate intervenes in the form of a bird of prey – see page 29)

'The Rat and the Oyster'
(see page 41)

'The Two Rats, the Fox and the Egg' (see page 40)

In The Philosophical Rat *by Edouard Lemoine, an elderly rat boosts the morale of his jaded young ward. He also helps out of pair of star-crossed lovers by eating the document that was preventing their marriage.*

Grandville's illustrations of the eponymous hero of The Philosophical Rat *show him thumbing his nose at a mechanical cat — and all the troubles of the world.*

An imprisoned rat is visited by his weeping family.

Here, the rich and greedy deny the poor rats any help.

Some Famous Literary Rats

Whittingtons Merchandize,
carried was to a land:
Troubled with Rats and Mice,
as they did vnderstand:
The King of that Contry there,
as he at dinner sat:
Daily remain'd in feare,
of many a Mouse and Rat.
Meat that on trenchers lay,
no way they could keepe safe:
But by Rats borne away,
fearing no wand nor staffe,
Whereupon soone they brought,
Whittingtons nimble cat:
Which by the King was bought,
heapes of gold giuen for that.

Richard Johnson,
'A Song of Sir Richard Whittington', 1612

… Two Rats crept up the Curtains, and ran smelling back-
wards and forward on the Bed: One of them came up
almost to my Face; whereupon I rose in a Fright, and drew
out my Hanger to defend my self. These horrible Animals
had the Boldness to attack me on both Sides, and one of
them held his Fore-feet at my Collar; but I had the good
Fortune to rip up his Belly before he could do me any
Mischief. He fell down at my Feet; and the other, seeing
the Fate of his Comrade, made his Escape, but not without
one good Wound on the Back, which I gave him as he
fled, and made the Blood run trickling from him … These
Creatures were of the Size of a large Mastiff, but infinitely
more nimble and fierce; so that if I had taken off my Belt
before I went to sleep, I must have infallibly been torn to
Pieces and devoured. I measured the Tail of the dead Rat,
and found it to be two Yards long, wanting an Inch …

Jonathan Swift, *Gulliver's Travels*, 1726

For many hours, the immediate vicinity of the low framework upon which I lay had been literally swarming with rats. They were wild, bold, ravenous; their red eyes glaring upon me, as if they waited but for motionlessness on my part to make me their prey.

'To what food,' I thought, 'have they been accustomed in the well?'...

(The prisoner lights upon the idea of coating his bindings in a grease that will be delicious to the rats. It works all too well ...)

Forth from the well they hurried in fresh troops. They clung to the wood – they overran it, and leaped in hundreds upon my person ... They pressed – they swarmed upon me in ever accumulating heaps. They writhed upon my throat; their cold lips sought my own; I was half stifled by their thronging pressure; disgust, for which the world has no name swelled my bosom, and chilled, with a heavy clamminess, my heart. Yet one minute, and I felt that the struggle would be over. Plainly I perceived the loosening of the bandage.

Edgar Allan Poe, 'The Pit and the Pendulum', 1842

Ratsbane:
Man against Rat

Human ingenuity has always enjoyed manufacturing ever more creative rat traps. Rats have been baited, drowned, starved, and electrocuted. The patron god of rat-killers is Apollo, who is said to have exterminated a whole swarm with his arrows.

One of the most enduring ways of dealing with rats is to curse them. Some have sworn by the Gospel of St John, read aloud in all corners of the home. Other cultures have devised respectful request formulas that urge the rats to leave. The Irish, with their gift of the gab, are said to be able to talk rats out of their homes.

In the event of a rat plague, one should pray to Saint Gertrude of Nivelles (626–59). This Belgian saint was the abbess of a monastery. She is usually depicted with a staff and a mouse or rat. Her cult spread from the Low Countries to Germany, England and beyond soon after her death.

In Ardennes in northern France it is said that a householder can clear his property of rats and even send them into an enemy's house by reciting the following: 'Erat verbum, apud Deum vestrum. Male rats and female rats, I entreat you in the name of Almighty God, to leave my house and all my habitations and go to such and such a place (inserting enemy's address if desired), there to end your days. Decretis, reversis et desembarassis virgo potens, clemens, justitiae.' The supplicant then has to write the same words on two pieces of paper, fold them up and place one under the door by which the rats are to leave and the other on the road that they are to take.

Never allow a rat
that can be killed to-day
to live till to-morrow.

Mark Hovell

A Rat-Removing Charm

I order all Rattons that be in this House,
All mannere of Rattons, and eke of Mouse,
By the grace of Mary cleane –
Go hence Rattons! and be no more seene –
And by Him, whom Mary bare aboute,
Let NO Ratton stay! within or withoute,
And by the Holy Ghost of grace,
That all Rattons! leave this place!
By the Father, and the Sone –
I bid all Rattons, to be Gone …

In the time of George II, England boasted a 'Rat-Killer to the Crown', who dressed in scarlet and gold livery with his own emblem of rats attacking some corn. He received a stipend of £100 a year, a not inconsiderable sum in those days.

The payment of small premiums for each rat caught has good results … In Denmark the rats were received at the fire stations; the tails of the rats brought in were cut off by the firemen, and the latter used them as their vouchers for the money they had paid out as premiums.

M.A.C. Hinton

The only way of dealing with the problem is by systematically organized 'ratting weeks'. This is a work in which the cooperation of that admirable organization, the Boy Scouts, might well be enlisted.

James Jenkins Simpson

73

The love of warmth brings many rats out of the sewers to take their siestas in the large hair warehouses in Lambeth … They have made runs up on the floors where the hair is placed to dry, and, finding a nice soft bit, roll themselves up quite into a ball; the outside of which is horse-hair, the nucleus a live rat. The boys connected with the establishment have found this out, and go feeling among the hair with their hands. The moment they come on a lump harder than the rest, they pounce upon it without fear, for the rat cannot bite through his thick self-made great-coat: they then rush off to a tub of water and shake poor Mr Rat out of his hairy (not downy) bed into the merciless element, when he is soon drowned.

Francis T. Buckland

When you wish to catch an ordinary rat, seize his tail, and lift him from the ground: at this instant he will try to turn up and bite, and a most severe bite he will give if you don't keep perpetually twisting him round and round – he then can't turn upwards; then having caught him in the right hand by the tail, swing him under the left arm. The rat will immediately endeavour to get away, and so doing fix himself on your waistcoat; bring your arm to your side, and you have him a prisoner.

Francis T. Buckland

When you have catched a Rat or a Mouse, cut or beat him severely, and let him go, and he will make such a crying noise, that his companions will leave the place. Some people flea off the skin of their heads: but this appears to be too cruel to practise.

The Complete Vermin Killer, 1777

Marcel Proust was said to enjoy watching rats being stabbed with hatpins.

   The usual complaint against rat-catchers, that
they take care not to ruin the stock, that they are
sure to leave breeders enough, could not be applied
to Sam … who, in this case, had evidently too much
delight in the chase himself, to dream of checking
or stopping it, whilst there was a rat left unslain.
On the contrary, so strong was the feeling of his
sportsmanship, and that of his poor curs, that one
of his grand operations, on the taking in of a
wheat-rick, for instance, or the clearing out of a
barn, was sure to be attended by all the idle boys
and unemployed men in the village … The grand
battue, on emptying Farmer Brookes's great barn,
will be long remembered in Aberleigh; there was
more noise made, and more beer drunk, than on any
occasion since the happy marriage of Miss Phoebe
and the patten-maker … The rats killed were in
proportion to the din – and that is a bold word too!
I am really afraid to name the number, it seemed to
myself, and would appear to my readers, so incredible.
Sam and Farmer Brookes were so proud of the
achievement, that they hung the dead game on the
lower branches of the great oak outside the gate.

Mary Russell Mitford, *Our Village*, 1824–32

Poison

Pison is also good for rats; it soften
their whole moral naturs.

Josh Billings

To the Powder of Arsenic (vulgarly
called Ratsbane) add fresh Butter,
made into a paste, with Wheat, or
Barley-meal and Honey. Spread pieces
of this mixture about those parts of the house they
mostly frequent: they will eagerly eat of it, and
when they have so done, will drink till they burst …

In Staffordshire it is
customary to put Bird-
lime about their holes,
and they running
among it, it will stick to
them so that they will not
leave scratching till they kill themselves …

Cork cut into small slices, and fried in Suet will
certainly kill them, if it be laid where they come …

If Hog's-lard be mixed with the brains of a Weasel
and distributed about a room, in bits as big as a nut,
they will not come hither.

The Complete Vermin Killer, 1777

One poisoned rat often kills more; his neighbours
eat his body, and
with it the poison.

Francis T. Buckland

All kinds of poisons have been used against the rat, but particularly phosphides: these give the rat a parching thirst that drives it out of the house in search of water; thus the homeowner avoids the stink of a dead rat behind the skirting boards. Other poisons contain violent laxatives.

Haec Fabula Docet

A rat who'd gorged a box of bane
And suffered an internal pain
Came from his hole to die (the label
Required it if the rat were able)
And found outside his habitat
A limpid stream. Of bane and rat
'Twas all unconscious; in the sun
It ran and prattled just for fun.
Keen to allay his inward throes,
The beast immersed his filthy nose
And drank – then bloated by the stream,
And filled with superheated steam,
Exploded with a rascal smell,
Remarking, as his fragments fell,
Astonished in the brook: 'I'm thinking
This water's damned unwholesome drinking!'

Ambrose Bierce (1842–1914?), American writer

They cared not a rap for the old-fashioned trap,
And they laughed at the dogs and the cats,
But with appetites keen, they ate some Rodine
And that was the end of the rats.

Advertisement for a Scottish rat-killer, 1929

Innocent method of destroying rats.
Lay bird lime in their haunts; for though they are
nasty enough in other respects, yet being very curious
of their fur, if it is but daubed with this stuff, it is so
troublesome to them that they will even scratch
their skins from off their own backs, to get it off,
and will never abide in the place where they suffered
in this manner.

The School of Arts or, Fountain of Knowledge, Containing Several Hundred Truly Valuable and Useful Receipts, Selected from the Works and Communications of the Most Eminent British Artists, 1810

Laid by the heels!

Cunning must be met by cunning. Rats, unless hunger-driven, are far too wary to venture the unaccustomed bait, poison-smeared and human-tainted; and too wily to enter the weird contraptions of wires and springs. Only the sticky trap of DAK is a match for the cunning of rats. Laid across the rat-run, it is unperceived until touched by a forefoot. The panicky struggle to free the imprisoned paw promptly lands the victim in the glutinous DAK, securely "laid by the heels." DAK clears premises and keeps them cleared for the traps retain their stickiness for many weeks. DAK catches mice literally by the dozen.

The rat's natural instinct is to die in privacy, if he can, and he generally, when poisoned, manages to get into a hole; there his body remains, and, as I know from personal experience, a dead rat in a room is by no means a pleasant subject, the odour proceeding therefrom being none of the nicest.

Francis T. Buckland

This reminds me of a plan adopted by a naturalist of an inventive genius, for discovering the exact position of a dead rat, the scent of which filled the entire room, and could not be traced to any particular spot. He closed the doors and windows of the room, caught half a dozen blue-bottle flies, and liberated them in the tainted room. Led by their instinct, they instantly flew to the spot where was lying the carcass of the rat, and by settling on the boards, indicated the exact spot where the dead rat lay.

John George Wood

Rat-Hunting Animals

There is scarcely any animal but what detests the rat, the dog will kill it without mercy, though he dislikes its flesh; nor will cats often eat any part but the head and then only when hungry, but the weasel is their most inveterate foe and being about its own size, follows it into its hole when a desperate fight is sure to take place always ending in favour of the weasel, for though the rat defends itself very valiantly the weasel catches hold, fastens, and sucks the blood at the same time, and so weakens its antagonist and obtains the victory.

J. Bland, *Grandpapa's Tales about Animals*, 1851

In Brazil rats have multiplied to such an extent that the inhabitants are obliged to train a certain kind of snake to exterminate them. This domestic snake is the giboia. When night comes on it makes its way to every part of the house with great caution and cunning. It even manages to creep up between the rafters of the roof and under the floor. If a rat appears it is doomed. With one bound the snake is upon it, catches it by the nape of the neck, and crushes it.

Alfred H. Miles

A rodent's chief mission in life is the unenviable one of providing food for other animals.

Arthur R. Thompson

If you be troubled with Irish *Rats*,
    Provide store of *Tartessian* Cats.

Robert Dixon, *Canidia*, 1683

An Ode to a Cat

A hungry Cat –
A foolish Rat.
    A lively Run –
    Exciting Fun.

Ferocious Jaws –
Remorseless Claws.
    A dying Squeal –
    A hearty Meal.

Alas, poor Rat!
O happy Cat!

Eugene Field (1850–95),
American poet

And when at night we venture forth to seek a little grain,
The dreaded Cat's eyes glance when we meet,
    which drives us back again.
With her four feet one spring she makes,
    with two claws holds and rears,
And once within her cruel grasp no plea for mercy hears;
Then with fierce mouth bites through the nape
    and carries off her prey,
Nor hears the poor Rat's agony, but quickly runs her way …
First she sniffs, next, gingerly the poor Rat's life blood tastes;
Then quickly gulps her nauseous feast – no particle she wastes.
Hearts, liver, guts, skin, tail and all, Oh! t'is a ghastly sight!
There's nothing of the poor Rat left, but his bones
    licked clean and bright.

Archibald John Little

Traps

On this page are illustrated just a few of the thousands of elaborate traps that have been devised for rats. But the rats continue to prosper, defying the traps, curses and poisons with feats of courage. A rat whose leg is caught in a sticky trap will often gnaw it off and limp away.

A rat-catcher in Vietnam recently won an environmental award for catching 200,000 rats with traps. He keeps their tails as souvenirs, recycling the corpses as food for pigs and dogs. His village is also trying to increase the cat population to combat the rats. Numbers of snakes (rats' main predator) have decreased in the area, because they are being hunted for meat to export to China.

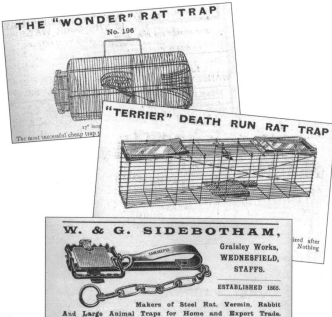

THE "WONDER" RAT TRAP

No. 196

17" long

The most successful cheap trap

"TERRIER" DEATH RUN RAT TRAP

ized after
Nothing

W. & G. SIDEBOTHAM,

Graisley Works,
WEDNESFIELD,
STAFFS.

ESTABLISHED 1865.

Makers of Steel Rat, Vermin, Rabbit
And Large Animal Traps for Home and Export Trade.

The best way tew domestikate them that ever I saw,
is tew surround them gently, with a steel trap; yu
kan reason with them then tew grate advantage …
Yu kan ketch them in allmoste enny kind ov trap
that haz got a way tew get into it.

Josh Billings

Sewers are usually infested, and it is naturally difficult
to cleanse them of rats. In those of Paris a means of
electrocuting them has been introduced; a live wire
is supported at a height of a few inches, and dainties
are hung at intervals above it. When a rat attempts
to snatch a morsel it puts its paw upon the wire, and
its existence is suddenly terminated. Boelter states
that the London sewers in the neighbourhood of
Soho are now free from rats
because of the quantities of
petrol which find their way
into the drains from the
motor works of that locality.

M.A.C. Hinton

Rat-Baiting

Rat-baiting was a popular sport in America and Great Britain in the mid-nineteenth century (along with bear-baiting). Rat-pits were lined with zinc or tin to prevent the animals climbing up the walls. Up to a hundred fit and feisty rats, collected by boys for a fee of five to twelve cents each, were dropped into the pit, followed by a single terrier dog (occasionally two dogs and two men). Sometimes the dog had to be rescued; other times it toiled for two hours to kill all the rats. One famous champion, known as Billy Underhill, killed a hundred rats in eleven and a half minutes. Henry Bergh, President of the American Society for the Prevention of Cruelty to Animals, tried to intervene and prosecute the rat-baiting entrepreneurs.

An English rat-baiting contest.

Laboratory Rats

Defenders of the rat will always cite the millions of rat lives given up in the name of science. The white laboratory rat is merely a Brown Rat bred to be albino.

Experiments on rats have revealed that they have neuroses of their own. Rats are afraid of new objects put in their path. This fear, of course, has served to protect them from traps. Rats also have their own sixth sense, named kinesthesis, which gives them an extra dimension of awareness, via their muscles.

The first laboratory rats went into space in 1950. NASA still puts experimental rats in space shuttles: over 700 rat astronauts have been sent into space. They have luxury cages but bedding is not required: they are floating in an environment without gravity. After a few hours they become dextrous at using their tails to steer. A strong airflow sucks their excrement straight into an exhaust system.

In October 2003, it was claimed that researchers succeeded in cloning two laboratory rats by nuclear transfer. Meanwhile, scientists have recently deciphered the full DNA sequence of the standard lab rat.

In Africa rats are being used to locate land mines. They are trained to sniff them out. They are harnessed and attached to a leash, then released onto an area where mines are believed to be buried. When the rat digs, indicating there is a mine in the ground, it is rewarded with a piece of banana. These African rats weigh around 1.35kg. As they are so light, they can run around minefields without the risk of setting the mines off – unlike dogs or humans.

Experiments with laboratory rats have shown that, if one psychologist in the room laughs at something a rat does, all of the other psychologists in the room will laugh equally. Nobody wants to be left holding the joke.

Garrison Keillor, *We Are Still Married*, 1989

Rat Lovers

Not everyone hates rats.

The Hindu god Ganesh is usually depicted with a rat at his feet. At the temple of the fifteenth-century mystic and healer Karni Mata, rats are still considered sacred, being the incarnations of the souls of her devotees. Worshippers bring offerings of food and milk for the swarming rodents at the temple near Bikaner in Rajasthan, and anyone who accidentally kills one by treading on it can only redeem his or her soul by replacing it with a life-size replica in pure gold.

Some rats allegedly make good-mannered and hygienic pets and performers. Albino rats have been kept as pets for nearly 300 years.

Susanna, Countess of Eglinton and her pet rats

This venerable woman amused herself latterly in taming and patronizing rats. She kept a vast number of these animals in her pay at Auchans, and they succeeded in her affections the poets and artists she had loved in early life. It does not reflect much credit upon the latter, that her ladyship used to complain of never having met with true gratitude except from four-footed animals. She had a panel in the oak wainscot of her dining-room, which she tapped upon and opened at meal times, when ten or twelve jolly rats came tripping forth, and joined her at table. At the word of command or a signal from her ladyship, they retired again to their native obscurity – a trait of good sense in the character and habits of the animals, which, it is hardly necessary to remark, patrons do not always find in two-legged protégés.

Robert Chambers, *Traditions of Edinburgh*, 1825

There was recently in Paris a Russian, by the name of Dourof, who is supposed to know more about the nature of rats than any other man living …

A reporter who visited M. Dourof and his two hundred and thirty free and ordinarily uncaged rats found him in the act of exhibiting his 'rat railroad'. It consisted of a narrow track laid in a circle, upon which were three passenger-cars large enough to hold five or six rats apiece, a baggage car, and a pretty little locomotive …

Presently a cage was brought in which was contained a considerable number of rats. Dourof clapped his hands together three times, and all the rats came tumbling out of the cage and swarmed into the station. He clapped his hands again, and half-a-dozen black and sleek rats – very respectable, corpulent fellows – climbed into the first car, which was a first-class coach. Once more Dourof clapped, and half-a-dozen black and white rats, quite regularly marked, got into the second-class car, while an indiscriminately marked and rather disreputable-looking company scrambled into the last car, which was third class.

A black rat, who did duty as the station-master, promenaded up and down on the platform of the little house, while two or three smaller rats dragged some trunks into the baggage-car. These were the 'baggage-smashers'. A whistle was heard; the engineer-rat climbed upon the locomotive, and a switchman rushed to the switch. Again the whistle sounded, and the train moved off around the track.

Alfred H. Miles

Talking of tame rats, I knew a worthy whipmaker who … had prepared a number of strips of leather, by well oiling and greasing them. He carefully laid them by in a box, but, strange to say, they disappeared one by one … one day, as he was sitting at work in his shop, a large black rat, of the original British species, slyly poked his head up out of a hole in the corner of the room … and ran straight to the box wherein were kept his favourite leather strips. In he dived, and quickly reappeared, carrying in his mouth the most dainty morsel he could find. Off he ran to his hole, and quickly vanished. Having thus found out the thief, the saddler determined to catch him. He accordingly propped up a sieve with a stick, and put a bait underneath; in a few minutes out came the rat again, smelling the inviting toasted cheese, and forthwith attacked it. The moment he began nibbling at the bait, down came the sieve, and he became a prisoner.

… The whipmaker at length lifted up the sieve, being armed with a stick ready to kill Mr Rat when he rushed out. What was his astonishment to see that the rat remained perfectly quiet, and, after a few moments, walk quietly up on his arm, and look up in his face, as much as to say, 'I am a poor innocent rat, and if your wife *will* lock up all the good things in the cupboard, why I must eat your nicely-prepared thongs; rats must live as well as whipmakers.' The man then said, 'Tom, I was going to kill you, but now I won't; let us be friends. I'll put you some bread and butter every day if you will not take my thongs and wax …'

Francis T. Buckland

This rat became so tame that it took to dozing on a window sill from which it was plucked and killed by a dog. The dog's master had it stuffed and mounted with a silver chain round its neck.

Rats on the Net

www.deadmentellnotales.com
You can buy a 12-inch plastic Bilge Rat here, among other accessories essential for pirates.

www.RatRescue.org
Home of the Rat Rescue Association and Mama Moondancer's Rattie Rescue. Care and adoption details, plus useful tips on how to take your rat to a motel etc.

www.rmca.org
The Rat and Mouse Club of America, estimates that there are 100,000 pet rat owners in the United States. Their site lists important events like 'RatFests' and 'Adopt A Rat' days. It also offers 'Cuisine des Rats', recipes for pet rats, and ideas on toys and other gifts.

www.identifont.com
The designer Noah Rothschild has created a quirky font called 'Rat Poison'.

www.arteveneziana.it/o/fiorellagallery
The site for Fiorella Mancini's Venetian rat fashion.

http://home.earthlink.net/~omniron/wr.html
A company called Vermin Brewing was founded in Chino, California, USA, in 1992. It produces beer; the company mascots are various rats that may be visited on the website. They also produce a newsletter, 'Wander Rat', featuring international destinations for rat tourists.

www.zoo-emmen.nl
The Noorder Dierenpark (zoo) in Emmen, Holland, has a special sewer rat exhibit, which includes a reconstruction of an arched brick Victorian sewer full of live rats, raised in laboratories. The male rats are given vasectomies rather than being sterilized, as the latter would affect their natural behaviour.

www.avonturenpark-hellendoorn.nl
At the Avonturenpark in Hellendoorn, also in Holland, you can ride the *Rioolrat* (sewer rat) rollercoaster. Each carriage is 'driven' by a human-sized model rat with a joy-stick.